Quaker relief work in Ireland's Great Hunger

1846-1849

ROBIN B. GOODBODY

GW00673821

QUAKER TAPESTRY BOOKLETS

1995

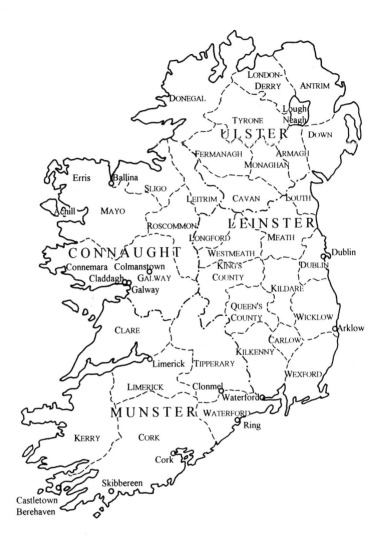

Ireland in the 1840s

Prologue

The famine that devastated Ireland in the late 1840s had its roots several generations before. Since the early to mid-eighteenth century the population had been growing at a rapid rate and by the 1840s more than eight million people inhabited the island – nearly double today's figure. Along with this, the bulk of the population came to depend increasingly on the potato as virtually the only food available to them. There were also faults in the land law that discouraged investment in farming and gave little security to most tenants, while the subdivision of holdings exacerbated the problem.

The famine, when it came, was not entirely unexpected. There had been severe problems before, resulting from bad weather conditions leading to poor harvests, and on several occasions the government and private agencies had embarked on relief measures. What was different in the autumn of 1845 was that a previously unknown disease struck the potato crop, destroying a significant amount of it in a very short time. The ensuing year of 1845/46 was one of major relief efforts by the government which on the whole were successful and were not all that different from those used on previous occasions.

Initial involvement

The food crisis that Ireland had faced after the crop failure in 1845 may not have been the worst that had ever occurred, but it was severe enough to have caused widespread concern. When the potato crop failed again in the autumn of 1846 it became evident that this was a more complete destruction and that over the ensuing months there would be a catastrophic shortage of food for large numbers of people. This led many individuals and groups to seek ways in which they could help and over time various organisations were set up to provide assistance.

Members of the Society of Friends, known to themselves as 'Friends' but more commonly known as 'Quakers', throughout Great Britain and Ireland were amongst those who were seeking ways of helping, and many individuals became involved in relief in their local areas. In addition, a number of Dublin Quakers discussed the idea of inviting members of the Society to unite their efforts to provide a more co-ordinated form of assistance. The first move came from Joseph Bewley, a member of the

Dublin Quaker family of tea merchants, who wrote to Irish Quakers at the beginning of November 1846 suggesting that Friends as a body should occupy their 'right place in any united effort that the emergency may require'. He went on to express a belief that the government relief measures would not solve the problem without the aid of individuals and local bodies and he sought comments on a proposal to set up a central committee to receive subscriptions, distribute funds and gather information.

His letter brought prompt replies which warmly encouraged the formation of a central committee of Quakers in Dublin. A meeting of men and women Quakers was called for 13 November at the Friends' meeting house at Eustace Street in Dublin 'for the purpose of considering what steps are proper to be taken by us towards the relief of the widely spread distress now existing in this country'.

The meeting agreed with the idea and appointed twenty-one Quakers to the new committee. From the start it was clear that the workload would be considerable and that it would be impractical to include anyone who did not live within easy reach of Dublin. Care was also taken to select those who had business interests that brought them into contact with various parts of the country where relief might be needed. To supplement this purely Dublin-based committee, another twenty-one Quakers were appointed corresponding members of the committee. Their function was to provide information and local contact.

A problem that faced this Central Relief Committee (CRC) from the outset was its centrality. To be able to meet frequently and function properly it had to be central and this meant, almost inevitably, in Dublin. By contrast, the areas worst hit by the crisis were widely dispersed and were predominately in those parts of the country furthest from Dublin. To add to this, the distribution of Quakers in Ireland was uneven and was at its lowest in the worst-hit areas, which were mainly in the west. The Society's organisation includes provincial meetings which are known as quarterly meetings as they meet four times a year. In Ireland there are three quarterly meetings for the provinces of Ulster, Munster and Leinster but there never has been one to cover the fourth province, Connaught, in the west. Within the provinces of Ulster and Munster there were no Quaker meetings in the western counties of Donegal, Fermanagh, Clare and Kerry.

Recognising this drawback, CRC saw one of its main functions as the gathering of information about the nature of the problem in different areas so that the best means might be found to alleviate it. The other objects were the more obvious ones of raising subscriptions and distributing relief.

The London Committee

At the same time as Quakers in Dublin met a similar meeting was convened in London. Whereas the initiative in Dublin had come from individuals, in London it came from Meeting for Sufferings (the standing representative body of British Quakers) which on 6 November 1846 had taken the decision to call a meeting to consider the matter. This took place on 9 November in London with a view to collecting information, organising the establishment of a subscription fund, to which members of the Society could contribute, and arranging for the funds to be distributed honestly and prudently. One of the principal decisions taken at that meeting was that Quakers in Ireland should be contacted in order to ask what they were intending to do and to seek advice as to what steps London Quakers could take.

The letter from the London meeting was received in Dublin in time to be considered at the first meeting of CRC immediately following the general meeting on 13 November. The reply informed London Quakers of the establishment of CRC and its network of correspondents and provided information on the extent of the suffering already occurring.

The London meeting was reconvened on 25 November in the light of the reply from Dublin and was attended by three members of the Dublin committee. At this meeting the decision was taken to establish a relief committee in London, and twenty Quakers were appointed to it.

The two committees were to work closely together during the ensuing crisis. To a large extent the London committee acted as a fund-raising body while its Dublin counterpart was involved in the distribution of relief. These were not hard and fast divisions, as the Dublin committee also raised funds while the London committee provided a great deal of additional assistance, including the collection of information through tours in the worst-hit areas by members of the committee. London Quakers also corresponded with the government on matters of policy, including proposals for the fisheries.

Addresses to members of the Society

One of the first tasks of each of the committees was to arrange for the writing, printing and distribution of 'addresses' to Quakers in their respective countries informing them of the establishment of the committees and seeking donations towards the relief efforts. The Dublin committee's address was completed on 30 November and the London address followed two days later.

CRC explained in its address that the efforts of government agencies to alleviate the distress were not being matched by the inhabitants of the affected districts. CRC felt that it was highly important that an example of energetic, united and well-directed effort by independent individuals of all classes should be more widespread than it actually was, and considered that the government measures could not be fully effective without private benevolence. Many Quakers had already set up relief measures in their own local areas. CRC urged that each Quaker should consider what he or she could do to help and that the work should be combined as far as possible into a united effort for greater effectiveness.

The London address set out the background to the problem in more detail and explained the extent to which many Irish people relied on the potato. To counter stories that there was plenty of food in Ireland the address explained that:

> many persons, when they reflect upon the stores of all kinds yet to be found in the ports and warehouses and markets of that fruitful island, deny the existence of famine altogether. But as famine may exist in one town or province, though plenty may be found elsewhere in the same kingdom; so famine may exist for one class of the community, whilst the rest may have, in adequate quantity, though at an increased price, of all the necessaries of life.

Moreover the existence of public relief works which paid wages could not solve the problem, as such works could assist only the able-bodied and could not hope to provide relief for many of those who were starving.

British Quakers were encouraged to donate liberally to the relief efforts and were reminded of 'the duties which the Divine law enjoins upon those who have towards those who have not'. The means of relief were to be through working closely with CRC and the hopes were that the efforts would not stop at direct relief to help the present crisis, but would look to the future by helping to bring about changes that would prevent this kind of catastrophe from happening again.

Tours

At the second meeting in London on 25 November 1846 William Forster, a Quaker from Norwich, offered to travel to Ireland to find out at first hand the extent of the distress, particularly in the remote districts. He had been working among the poor of Norwich where he had gained a great deal of experience in running soup kitchens. He intended to advise on the setting up of these establishments as well as investigating suitable channels for directing relief to the worst hit areas and establishing the best ways of offering relief. With the encouragement of London Quakers he set out for Dublin the very next day and was joined on the way by Joseph Crosfield, a Quaker merchant from Liverpool.

William Forster met with CRC on 30 November and was given the authority to draw on its funds along his route in order to give direct financial grants wherever he felt it necessary. Over the next four and a half months he travelled in Ireland accompanied by a succession of companions. These included his son William Edward Forster, who would later become the Chief Secretary for Ireland, and James Hack Tuke of York, who would return to undertake his own tour. Forster's tour brought him through counties Roscommon, Leitrim, Fermanagh, Donegal, Sligo, Mayo, Galway, Longford and Cavan. Throughout his travels he and his companions kept in constant contact by letter with CRC.

Some of these letters were published by CRC as part of its policy for making known the extent of the famine and increasing public awareness of the problem. These extracts tell of large numbers of destitute labourers working on relief schemes and of people who had had little or nothing to eat for a considerable time. A visit to a poor-house, or workhouse, early in their tour found:

> poor wretches in the last stage of famine imploring to be received into the house; women who had six or seven children begging that even two or three might be taken in ... some of these children were worn to skeletons, their features sharpened with hunger, their limbs wasted almost to the bone.

This scene reflected the absence of any legal right to relief under the Irish poor law. Under this law the country was divided into districts known as poor law unions, each of which was looked after by an elected board of guardians and they had no obligation to offer assistance once the poor house was full to capacity.

Over the next year or so many Quakers from both Ireland and England toured the country, and usually the reports they presented were published in order to keep public awareness alive. Some of these journeys were for specific tasks, such as to investigate reports of particular distress or to check on relief operations, but others were for more general gleaning of information and making of contacts.

Relief

As William Forster set out on his tour CRC was considering how best to operate. An office was rented in Dublin and a clerk engaged. A sub-committee was set up to administer the requests for assistance. Its terms of reference required it to meet at least three times a week and to sit daily if the work load required it.

CRC recognised that its resources would be extremely limited in comparison with the enormous crisis which was looming, and decided that value for money would be an important part of a decision to grant relief: care was to be taken to avoid duplicating relief measures provided by other agencies, including government relief works. CRC also stipulated that any project which was aided by the Quaker committees would be strictly non-sectarian, and would make no preference in the distribution of relief on the grounds of religious profession. At the end of the famine the committee felt it was able to state that 'there is reason to believe that the cases were few in which this condition was not faithfully observed'. This was in contrast with the actions of a number of evangelical missionaries who had been attempting to convert the populace away from the Catholic faith and who made a name for themselves during the famine by using food as a means of enticing people to change their religion.

Soup kitchens

One of the main ways in which Quakers assisted the hungry was through soup kitchens. These were often set up by individual Quakers or Quaker families or groups in their own local areas. In most cases these are now forgotten, though in some instances something of the story survives through reports in the media or minute books of the organising committee. One of the earliest soup kitchens established by Quakers was set up in Waterford in the autumn of 1846 and others included Clonmel, Carrick-on-Suir, Mountmellick, Ferns and Enniscorthy. Quakers in Cork also established a soup kitchen and this became one of the best known, as it was pictured in the *Illustrated London News* in January 1847, becoming one of the most widely reproduced illustrations of the famine period.

In Dublin CRC opened a soup kitchen in Charles Street in January 1847 for the dual purpose of giving relief to the poor and acting as a model for the provision of soup kitchens elsewhere. As a result of experience there cooked rice was introduced as it had been found that a purely liquid diet was causing bowel problems.

The soup shops were in operation until the summer of 1847. New government relief measures had come into force in the spring which encouraged the poor law unions to set up soup kitchens as the official means of relief during the summer of that year. As a result, the number of people attending the Quaker soup kitchens fell substantially until it was no longer practical to keep them open. The soup shop in Dublin closed on 22 July 1847, though the premises were kept for a period in case it became necessary to reopen.

In line with much Quaker relief work the soup on offer was not given

Quaker soup kitchen in Cork, January 1847

away free of charge, but was sold at a modest price. This avoided pauperising the recipients while at the same time offering good, nourishing food at a price which was reasonable. Tickets could be bought by charitable organisations and individuals for distribution to the poor, thereby involving others in the scheme and ensuring that those without money did not go hungry. In Dublin two alternatives were offered. A quart of soup could be had on its own at a cost of a penny, while for an extra halfpenny bread would be included. These prices represented a loss to CRC as it was calculated that it would cost 6½d. per gallon to produce the soup, including management costs, while the sales would only bring a return of 4d. per gallon.

Over the six months of its operation the Charles Street soup shop dispensed more than a hundred thousand quarts of soup and, in its early days, the amount came to an average of a thousand quarts of soup per day. In all, the operation cost CRC £300, which was less than a third of the turnover of the soup shop, so that the £300 donation purchased £917 worth of assistance to the hungry. At today's prices this represents relief to the value of £50,000 at a cost of £16,500. The Waterford soup kitchen was serving more than seven hundred people five times a week in February 1847 and also supplied a thousand straw beds. In Cork the auxiliary committee's soup kitchen averaged almost 1,400 quarts of soup a day in late February 1847.

Auxiliary Committees

CRC began by handling all of the requests for relief itself. This soon became too large a task for it and some of the power was devolved to more locally based committees. As there was no concentration of Quakers in the province of Connaught, nor in the western part of Ulster, this system of local committees operated only in Munster.

In December 1846 CRC asked Quakers in Cork to investigate reports of great distress in the town of Skibbereen in the west of the county and three of them set out to check the facts. Cork Friends set up their own committee to look after this matter and raised £54 for Skibbereen while CRC sent a further £300. Skibbereen became one of the best known areas which suffered during the famine, and in February 1847 Friends were told that the town was:

one mass of famine, disease and death; the poor creatures hitherto trying to exist on one meal per day, are now sinking under fever and bowel complaints – unable to come for their soup, and this not fit for them: rice is what their whole cry is for; but we cannot manage this well, nor can we get the food carried to the houses from dread of infection.

At Munster Quarterly Meeting in January a special session to consider relief measures was attended by Joseph Bewley of CRC. He put forward a proposal that auxiliary committees be set up in Waterford, Clonmel and Limerick on the lines of that already operating in Cork. The four would operate as auxiliary committees of CRC in Dublin on the basis that Dublin would provide funding while the assessment of applications for relief would be done by the local organisations.

CRC set down the boundaries of the areas to be covered by the four auxiliary committees. Each of these would be large, encompassing several counties. The Cork committee was to look after all of Cork and most of Kerry, together with part of Waterford. The Waterford committee would concern itself with much of Waterford along with Kilkenny and Wexford. Clonmel would handle the remaining part of Waterford and most of Tipperary. Limerick was to have responsibility for Limerick and Clare along with parts of Kerry, Tipperary and Galway. In all, these committees were given charge of not just the province of Munster but also the Leinster counties of Kilkenny and Wexford and part of the Connaught county of Galway: through their work, the auxiliary committees took a great deal of pressure off CRC.

Fund raising

None of the measures undertaken by CRC could have been contemplated without significant funding. The necessary money came in the first instance from Quakers themselves, beginning with about £1,700 offered by those who attended the initial meeting in Dublin in November 1846, representing over £90,000 at today's values. By early December the London committee had received a further £3,000 in subscriptions and in January an additional £5,000 was sent from London to Dublin.

Once CRC published its address in Ireland in December 1846 copies were sent to Jacob Harvey, a Friend in New York, who set in train moves to seek funds from American Quakers. In January 1847 the London committee wrote to Quakers in North America describing the state of Ireland and its prospects for the ensuing year. Having described how committees had been set up in Dublin and London and were working towards the alleviation of suffering, the address reminded American Quakers of the abundance of the recent harvests on that continent and invited them to send food or money to aid the relief work.

The first response received from America was £500 which arrived from Philadelphia in January. Towards the end of January a public meeting was called in that city chaired by the Chief Justice of the Supreme Court and a few days later another public meeting was held in Washington chaired by the Vice-President of the United States, George Mifflin Dallas, who was from Philadelphia. From these beginnings the collection of funds in America grew to enormous proportions and encompassed a wide geographical area and a great variety of donors.

One of the early problems Ireland had found in seeking support from America was that accounts in the media frequently played down the extent of the crop failure, giving the impression that it was partial and that, as in the previous year, official relief measures would be able to cope. The information sent by Quakers in Dublin and London helped to correct this impression and to give a more reliable picture of just how bad matters were.

From the initial sum received in January donations from America began to pour in and ultimately almost £16,000 in subscriptions was entrusted to CRC in Dublin. This was not entirely without controversy, such as when subscriptions were received from places involved in slavery which was anathema to the Society of Friends.

As part of its publicity campaign CRC published 5,000 copies of extracts from correspondence with America following two similar extracts of other correspondence published in January and March 1847.

Donations

While the money donated to the relief committees was welcome and extremely useful it formed only a fraction of the total value of donations. Some individuals and organisations gave whatever goods they could manage, including a gift of a full set of Ordnance Survey maps of the counties of Ireland from the Dublin booksellers of Hodges & Smith in January 1847.

The main bulk of non-monetary donations came in food. Allied with food donations came generous assistance with freight and other help – a considerable amount of this came from the government. In February 1847 the London committee urged that food ought to be distributed more liberally in the remote parts of the west and north-west of Ireland. The lack of any established means of transport to these areas led the London committee to approach the government for help. Assistance was granted in the form of the loan of two steamships, the *Albert* and the *Scourge*. These ships sailed from Liverpool in that month and delivered cargoes of rice, peas, Indian meal, biscuit and American beef to a number of ports along the west coast. Along with these food cargoes were boilers for soup. Fifty of these were donated by the Coalbrookdale Quaker iron manufacturers Alfred Darby and his brother Abraham IV.

As with the monetary donations the great majority of food supplies came from America. The first of these was a ship named the *Victor* which arrived from New York in mid-April with a cargo of Indian meal. Within three weeks an estimated twenty ships had left America with further cargoes. Within America freight, storage and railway companies gave their services free of charge to any package labelled 'Ireland'. Once the goods reached the American ports the cost of shipping the supplies to Ireland was paid by the government of the United Kingdom.

CRC's final report, or *Transactions*, described how 'ships of war approached our shores, eagerly seeking not to destroy life but to preserve it; their guns being taken out in order to afford more room for stowage'. In view of the Quaker testimony against war this statement suggests that CRC saw how, for a brief moment, swords were being beaten into ploughshares.

In all, it is estimated that the food donated from America amounted to ninety-one shipments containing almost 10,000 tonnes with a value of £100,000. On top of this, the government paid the bill for shipping amounting to £33,000.

Clothing donations

During times of famine clothing is almost as necessary for the maintenance of life as food. The severity of the winter of 1846/47 made this all the more critical, particularly as the destitute in Ireland sold or pawned clothing to get money for food.

The move to provide clothing came from Britain, particularly from English women Friends who encouraged women's groups throughout the country to set up their own efforts for collecting and making clothes. Donations of clothing bound for Ireland were carried free of charge by the railway companies in Britain and by the Irish shipping companies. In January 1847 CRC received several bales of clothing and established a subcommittee to look after the storage and distribution, working in conjunction with a women's committee of Dublin Quakers. The subcommittee took on premises with space for bulk storage of clothing and it employed three clerks, a packer and a boy, with other help being added during busy periods.

Ready-made clothing was received from Britain and America as well as cash donations, and the subcommittee used its funds to purchase fabrics for distribution to suitable bodies which were providing employment in manufacturing clothing for the needy. Leather was provided for the manufacture of shoes as it was found that labourers often could not work on the government relief schemes because of a lack of footwear. The clothing distributed was welcomed by the needy, though the quantities arriving were usually insufficient, as one Quaker reported after witnessing the distribution of a bale of clothing:

> The difficulty of selection was very great, where the supply, though so good and serviceable, was but a drop in the rolling ocean of destitution and nakedness.

By July 1847 the amount of clothing arriving was down to a trickle and it was decided to wind up the clothing subcommittee. By this time it had handled two hundred and ten bales of clothing and more than £1,800 in cash, together with a subsidy of £650 from CRC. A total of nearly seven hundred grants of clothing had been made, spread through all thirty-two counties of Ireland.

As winter approached again the problem of inadequate clothing once more became an issue and in November 1847 a new clothing subcommittee was established. This time it concentrated on fabrics rather than ready-made clothing so as to be able to facilitate the giving

14

of employment. Grants from the clothing subcommittee were given on the basis that where possible the value should be repaid out of the earnings of the recipients. Only a fraction of the expenditure could be recovered in this way, but it ensured that of the total of almost £6,300 given by CRC some £1,300 was repaid. Over and above this, the auxiliary committees in Munster made grants of clothing, as did a ladies' association in Dublin.

Distribution of relief

From the outset it was evident that it would not be a simple matter to assist all those in need. CRC did not see itself as attempting to feed the starving directly, but merely to provide the food and money for others to do it. Most of the members of CRC were merchants and this gave them the necessary skills for distributing large amounts of supplies which would be handed over to local people of means such as the gentry, clergy, businessmen, professional classes and their families who would set up local relief committees.

Wherever Quakers were to be found in Ireland, they tended to become involved in this local distribution through measures such as soup kitchens. However, the number of Quakers in Ireland was small and they could not hope to make a major impact on their own, particularly as they did not live in the worst hit areas.

A further problem was that the merchant classes, the gentry and the professional classes were also thin on the ground in the hardest hit areas so that in many places there was no one who could take the responsibility for carrying out voluntary relief work. Commerce was also poorly developed in these areas and in many parts of the west of Ireland there was no established network of merchants and traders through whom supplies could be bought by local relief agencies. Information about these more remote areas was lacking and one of the most vital tasks carried out in the tours by William Forster and other Friends was to establish contact with suitable people who could be encouraged to form relief committees and act as agents on the ground for the distribution of relief.

Once it became publicly known that Quakers had set up committees to provide relief, applications started to come in from all over the country. Each applicant was required to submit the request on the committee's

Jonathan Pim, one of the secretaries of the Central Relief Committee
and later a Member of Parliament

application form which was also designed to glean information about the state of the district for which relief was sought. The questions included topics such as population, extent of destitution, nature of farming and fisheries, unemployment rates, amount of government and private relief already under way, health of the populace, current prices of foodstuffs and the levels of food stocks in the district. Finally, the form sought the name of a referee in Dublin who could be consulted as to the state of the district and the qualities of the applicants.

Once CRC was satisfied that the applicant was suitable and that there was a genuine need for relief a grant could be made. In the first instance grants of about £10 to £20 were made on the basis that further instalments could be advanced once the recipient had shown that the funds were being used effectively. In this way waste and misuse of funds was minimised. The preferred means of relief was through soup kitchens and to this end almost three hundred soup boilers were distributed to almost every county in Ireland.

As time progressed, the number of applications overwhelmed CRC despite the assistance given by the auxiliary committees. A subcommittee was set up to manage things more efficiently, with individual members being given specific tasks and each of the provinces of Ulster, Leinster and Connaught was allocated to four members.

When the ships laden with American food began to arrive, there was a need to organise a system for moving the food from the port of landing to its destination. This was not an easy matter as transport was poorly developed, particularly in some of the more remote areas. At this time the railway network in Ireland was in its infancy and there were few lines. The carriage of food wagons through the country was fraught with danger as travel to virtually any destination involved passing through places where there was severe hunger and on occasions mobs attacked food convoys. As Quakers were opposed to the use of arms concern was expressed at their Yearly Meeting in Dublin in the spring of 1847:

> that Friends in the country who were concerned in the transportation of flour, or other provisions, should be careful not to avail themselves of the protection of armed police.

On top of the transportation problem was that of storage. Large amounts of provisions required extensive warehousing and this could be needed at short notice in whatever port an American ship arrived.

The solution came through an arrangement with the government's

Commissariat which by this time had a network of food depots throughout the country. As these were set up specifically to assist famine relief they were located so as to enable food to be brought to the right places. Under the arrangement all food supplies which arrived in Irish ports bound for CRC would be transferred to the Commissariat and lodged in its depots. In exchange, CRC received a credit note to the value of the food at the current market price and could then use this credit to draw supplies from depots anywhere in the country. This meant that a consignment reaching Cork could be used to relieve hunger in, say, Donegal, almost instantaneously despite the great distance.

Throughout the distribution of relief CRC was eager to ensure that local trade was not undermined. The famine affected more than just the poorest level of society and spread through the entire economy. Rents were not paid so there was a severe reduction in the income of landlords and their spending power was reduced. When added to the lack of spending of the tenants, this led to a general reduction in trade. Houses were not built or repaired so that masons, carpenters and other tradesmen suffered, as did tailors and shoemakers through the fall in the demand for clothing, and the gentry had to cut down on the number of labourers and servants they employed. CRC recognised that, if it brought large amounts of flour into an area, it would, by bypassing the local flour merchant, jeopardise his business and threaten the jobs of his employees. This would mean that, once the crisis was over, these businesses would not be there to help local trade back to normal. In order to overcome this, CRC tried to avoid supplying food to an area if that type of food was already available locally.

Distribution of seed

The blight had caused a great deal of damage to the potato crop when it first appeared in the autumn of 1845 and had virtually wiped it out in 1846. Quakers were not alone in realising that the potato could no longer be trusted to feed so many people and that the food shortage following the destruction of the crop ensured that there were very few potatoes left as seed for the 1847 sowing. The solution to these problems was to supply alternative seed, and in view of the lack of knowledge of other crops it was also necessary to teach the basics of growing the alternatives.

The first initiative came from an English Quaker, William Bennett, who arrived in Dublin in March 1847 and announced to CRC that he was about to set out to the remote parts of Ireland to distribute seeds for green crops. He acquired supplies of seeds in Dublin, mainly concentrating on turnip, swede, carrot and mangel-wurzel with additional quantities of flax, parsnip and cabbage. He and one of his sons travelled to Mayo and Donegal and distributed seeds there with apparently successful results, though in some cases the seeds were planted too densely.

In the same month, the Waterford auxiliary committee granted some seed to some small farmers in the south of county Wexford. CRC was apprehensive about seed distribution. Many small farmers had fallen seriously in arrears with their rent as a result of the failure of the potato crop and there was a strong possibility that any crops which might be grown would be confiscated by the landlord to offset the rent arrears. In the case of the Wexford farmers this was not an issue as they were, in effect, freeholders.

Towards the end of May 1847 CRC was given some 40,000 lbs – or more than eighteen tonnes – of green crop seeds by the government. A member of the committee undertook to arrange the distribution of these seeds. Using the postal system together with the help of free transport donated by a coach company and a steampacket company, he made more than 40,000 grants of seeds which were estimated to have resulted in the sowing of nearly 10,000 acres and raising nearly 200,000 tonnes of turnips.

In the following year, 1848, CRC took on this method of relief again and increased its quantity to more than sixty tonnes of seeds. This was granted to nearly 150,000 persons and more than 32,000 acres were sown. Before each grant was made, a local correspondent verified that the applicants were really in need of assistance and that the ground had been properly prepared.

Changes in government relief

From the autumn of 1846 to the spring of 1847 the government relief was based on employing labourers on work projects such as building roads. For the really destitute the poor-houses could offer relief once the person was admitted as an inmate. This was a dramatic move which involved giving up any landholding and splitting up the family as in the poor houses inmates were segregated by age and sex. During much of the famine period the poor-houses were full to capacity and many people were unable to gain entry. Yet the law did not permit the guardians of the poor law unions to provide relief to people who were not inmates.

By March 1847 the numbers of people employed on the government relief works had reached almost three quarters of a million, representing about three million people including dependants, or more than a third of the population. The wages offered were not sufficient to enable people to purchase adequate food and the rate of starvation was on the increase.

At this point the government changed its policy, deciding to end the employment on the relief works and replacing this system by introducing a network of soup kitchens to be operated by the local guardians of the poor law unions and set up within each electoral division. Much of the work of the Society of Friends involved assisting the establishment and operation of soup kitchens, but the introduction of government soup kitchens would render their contribution unnecessary. However, CRC could see that the establishment of soup kitchens in the poor law unions could not be done overnight and that the reduction of employment on the relief works would proceed faster than the alternative could be brought into play. The decision was taken, therefore, to continue to supply food as an interim measure to cover the gap between the finish of one government measure and the start of the next.

With the prospect of the provision of food becoming unnecessary, CRC decided that it should become involved with the poor law unions in distributing relief. With the co-operation of the government CRC sent questionnaires to the government officers in the unions to ascertain the extent of destitution and an approach was made to the government to seek funds to match those that Quakers could provide. However, the government was not willing to back the idea and the replies to the questionnaires showed that the extent of destitution was so bad that Quakers could not hope to make a realistic contribution.

For a time, however, CRC found that the ending of employment on the relief works was increasing the numbers who needed to be fed at the soup kitchens. It was fortunate that at this point the ships began to arrive with supplies from America. From March until June 1847, the Quaker relief work acted at a very intensive level. After that, however, operations could be scaled down. They reached a low level by July when over three million people were being fed daily by the government.

By the autumn of 1847 CRC had greatly reduced its involvement in the distribution of food because of the government measures and because the remaining funds available were not sufficient to allow for any large scale continuance of this form of relief. Further grants were confined to those who were still not eligible for government assistance, including the sick, the old and the infirm, while CRC became involved in new directions. However, the amounts of relief were still significant and the weekly grants of food amounted to anything from twenty to seventy tonnes until August 1848 when it slowed down to a trickle. At the same time the stock in hand of provisions fell from over 3,000 tonnes in February 1848 to twelve tonnes at the end of the year. With the winding down of food distribution and the concurrent closure of the government food depots it was decided that the remaining food should be sold to the Commissariat, and significant amounts of the stock were sold from time to time throughout the year. As a result, CRC received some £37,500 which became available for new projects.

A year later, in July 1849, the system of grants for food was reactivated briefly at the behest of the London committee as destitution had reached crisis level again following the loss of the potato crop in 1848. Grants were made over a period of a few weeks until the new harvest reduced the scale of the crisis once more.

Emigration

Almost as many people emigrated from Ireland during the famine as died. The Quaker committees in Ireland were not involved with the assistance of emigrants but Quakers elsewhere worked hard to help those who were arriving in a new country, often in poor physical condition, with very little money and few prospects. Jacob Harvey in New York was the principal contact in America for the relief committees in Britain and Ireland. He worked extremely hard to ensure that the donations of American relief continued to go to Ireland. He also worked long hours with the Irish immigrants who were pouring into New York and he eventually broke his health through overwork and died in the spring of 1848.

In later years James Hack Tuke, who had toured the west of Ireland on behalf of the relief committees in 1847, became closely involved in schemes for assisting emigration from Ireland to enable people to begin new lives in other countries.

Employment

Throughout its relief operations, CRC recognised that the distribution of food was an emergency measure that would not change matters for the better in the long term. In fact, Quakers shared the prevailing view that the giving of gratuitous relief was ultimately bad for the recipient.

The change in government policy regarding relief allowed Quakers to become involved in measures which they considered would have greater long term effects, notably the provision of employment. There followed a variety of projects aimed at producing medium to long term benefits, including the distribution of seed already mentioned. Assistance was also given to industrial schools which were seen as having the dual benefit of instructing children in useful industrial skills as well as feeding them.

Financial aid was given to a number of industrial undertakings, mainly through loans. These included kelp processing in Donegal and an abortive scheme for a woollen manufactory in Mayo. Over time CRC was involved in a number of larger scale projects including fisheries and agriculture. Other Quakers were also providing jobs, such as the manufacture of cheap clothing set up by women Friends in Cork early in 1847.

Fisheries

During a crisis, such as the Irish famine, articles tend to be sold or pawned in order to get money for food and these often include the very equipment needed for obtaining an income. On his journey in Connaught early in 1847 William Forster found that the fishermen in the tight-knit community of the Claddagh in Galway were unable to put to sea as they had pawned their nets and had no money to repair their boats. He made grants to them to remedy this.

In the spring of 1847 the auxiliary relief committee in Waterford was approached for assistance by James Alcock, vicar of Ring in the west of that county. That committee made available loans to enable the fishermen to redeem or replace their nets and fishing gear. For the most part these loans were repaid. Grants were made for the purchase of boats and hemp for nets and for the encouragement of new fishing methods. Also in Ring the auxiliary committee became involved in a scheme for establishing a fish curing factory and some £200 was advanced for this purpose. The enterprise ran for a year and provided much needed employment in the district, but it closed for reasons not connected with the viability of the plant and a promising project came to an end. The fisheries continued to thrive and the loans from the auxiliary committee effectively kept this fishing community intact without the decimating effects of starvation or emigration.

Following its move away from food relief, CRC began to encourage fishing as an industry, particularly in the west. Loans were given to fishermen in various places such as Arklow, Dunmore East, Kingstown and Ballycotton, but the main effort went toward setting up fishing stations at various points around the west coast.

Four of these stations were established, at Ballinakill Bay near Clifden in Galway, Achill Sound and Belmullet in Mayo and Castletown, Berehaven in Cork. A fish curing plant was also set up at Castletown in an effort to make the most of the catch which would be landed there. Neither Ballinakill Bay nor Achill Sound managed to get properly established and the other two stations were deemed unprofitable after only a year. The problem with these schemes was seen by CRC as one of basic organisation, as it was felt that they could not be run properly by a Dublin-based committee and needed private enterprise which was not forthcoming. In view of the large expenditure on Castletown and the numbers of people dependent on it for employment the management was restructured and it lasted another three years.

The nature of the investment in these fisheries may be seen through the example of Belmullet. A sum of three hundred pounds was made available to a single individual who was to remain responsible for it. With this he purchased fifteen boats along with the requisite nets, lines and other equipment at a cost of £14-10s-0d. per boat. He also bought ten curraghs at £4 each and spent £42-10s-0d. on equipment for them, enabling some eighty to a hundred fishermen to return to work. The loan was secured on the boats and tackle and they were to remain the property of CRC until the loan was repaid, after which the ownership would transfer to the crew according to a formula set down by CRC. This enterprise was established in November 1847 and continued until October 1849 when CRC wound up the operation on the grounds of mismanagement by the proprietor.

At Castletown some fifty-four men were employed on nine boats, but the location was not ideal for fishing. The distance to the fishing grounds was as much as twenty-five miles, bait was not readily available and suitable provisions for taking to sea could not be purchased locally. After two years in operation the nature of the fishery was changed to make better use of its location, but by 1852 it was obvious that there was no future in the concern as it could not be self-supporting.

In December 1847 CRC agreed to acquire a trawler to service the smaller fishing boats and help them to return to port when bad weather appeared. There was some doubt about the real need for this service but CRC went ahead and leased a 55-ton trawler along with crew and fishing gear. The boat had not been long in Castletown when it became obvious that the doubts were well founded and that it was serving little purpose. In anticipation of this CRC had ensured that the trawler was equipped to make fishing trips on its own and to explore the west coast while doing so. This alternative did not produce any useful result as the almost complete lack of any reliable charts of the waters off the west coast made it difficult to operate. Much time was wasted by the crew taking their own soundings. Even so the fishing gear was constantly snagged and damaged on the bottom which invariably proved to be rocky.

In the spring of 1848 the London committee (see minute reproduced opposite), in conjunction with the Limerick auxiliary committee, began a programme to assist the fishermen in the Claddagh to advance the temporary relief provided to them by William Forster a year before. They engaged a Cornish fishing expert, redeemed equipment from pawn again, established a fish curing plant and attempted to introduce more modern methods of fishing. However, the very conservative fishing community was resistant to many of the changes and ultimately the attempts had to be abandoned.

During the famine it was often said that the waters around Ireland were teeming with fish while the people starved. It was this that led CRC to support fishing efforts. Ultimately, none of the major schemes undertaken by CRC succeeded in supplying employment in the long term. It is important, though, that each of these projects provided much needed

At a Meeting of the Irish Relief Committee
held 16th of 5th month 1849

A communication is now received from
Darcy on behalf of the Committee having the
management of the curing house at Galway
giving an encouraging account of the progress
of the business of the curing house and stating
the desirableness of a good boat being sent out to
introduce improved methods of deep-sea fishing.
This Committee is desirous of promoting the object
and refers the subject to the care of George Stacey
& John Hodgkin (to whom the correspondence with
Galway has been already committed) with the
assistance of Jos.h G. Barclay and of Henry Christy
(if he be willing to join them) and they are re-
-quested to make enquiries with a view to ascertain
the best method of assisting in sending out a
boat as requested by the Galway Committee & they
are authorized to expend any sum not exceeding
£ 300 in such manner as they may think fit
in promoting the object.

(copy &Al)

Copy of minute of the London committee relating to the fisheries at the
Claddagh, May 1849

food and employment at the time when it was particularly needed and the lesser projects, such as the grants given to the more established fisheries, certainly saved these fishing communities from total ruin. Of all the fishery projects, Ring emerges with the greatest measure of success, the fishermen being able to carry on their operations from their own resources once given the initial boost.

Agriculture

Some of the largest scale projects undertaken by CRC were designed to help agriculture to recover from the effects of the famine and the reliance on the potato. In keeping with the tenets which are still encouraged by modern relief workers, the first projects were intended to introduce new methods using readily available and well-established implements and skills. The traditional Irish method of growing potatoes and many other crops was by spade cultivation. CRC considered that this labour-intensive system could be worked on a large scale to provide productive jobs, produce food and teach the cultivation of new crops.

Early in 1848 an area on the border of counties Mayo and Sligo was selected for a major project incorporating cultivation by spade labour. Arrangements were made with several landowners to manage more than thirty farms spread over an area some twelve miles by fourteen miles and including a total of 900 statute acres, to be given free of rent for a year.

As this scheme progressed, more than a thousand people were given work preparing the land for crops. In selecting the crops to be sown, the potato was not to be used and the choice was otherwise based on the best that could be managed with spade labour and using the minimum input of manure. It was felt that purchasing manure locally would deprive the other landholders of their needs by distorting the market and so fertilisers such as guano were bought from merchants. Wages were based on the amount of work carried out, but were higher than normal to allow for the fact that the workers were generally weakened by the starvation of the previous seasons.

In July the crops were coming close to maturity and two Quakers were asked to inspect the scheme and report to CRC. Their report was less than encouraging. They found that the enterprise had suffered from the start because the land had been neglected for a time and had never been properly cultivated. The turnips had been attacked by fly and had to be resown two or even three times. The peas and beans were imperfectly cultivated and other crops such as parsnips, carrots and flax were behind in their growth and would not produce a good crop. Attempts to grow grains had been a total failure. They recommended that a qualified supervisor be appointed without delay to oversee the remainder of the project and this was done.

At the end of the experiment, the sale of the crops came nowhere near covering the costs of the exercise, but CRC felt that it was not a complete failure as it had provided wages for large numbers of people at a time of real need and it had taught them how to cultivate alternatives to the potato. A further benefit was that in the following year two industrial ventures went ahead in the area with loans from CRC: these were based on the introduction of flax into the area in the previous year's experiment.

This was the largest of the spade labour schemes assisted by CRC, but it was not the only one. A loan was extended to a landowner in county Galway to reclaim fifty acres into cultivation in 1848 and in the following year one of the major landowners involved in the Ballina spade cultivation experiment was lent £800 to bring a hundred acres of waste into cultivation and this sum was also repaid. A similar scheme in county Fermanagh brought about the cultivation of fifty acres.

The most ambitious agricultural project was the model farm which CRC established in 1849. The suggestion came from Dr. Edward Bewley, a Quaker from Moate in Westmeath, who approached CRC in August 1848, just as the Ballina experiment was drawing to a close. He produced a more detailed plan for the project in September proposing the purchase of a farm of about 325 statute acres. The scheme was approved by CRC and five members of the committee were detailed to find a suitable property. Over the months the details were worked out more thoroughly, and Edward Bewley visited England and Scotland where he inspected various farms run by Quakers. Meanwhile, the acquisition of a farm was not proving easy as, despite the state of the country, no farm seemed to be available to suit the purpose, but by mid February a site had been found in the eastern part of county Galway.

The land was at Colmanstown, not far from the town of Athenry, and at 675 statute acres it was more than double the size envisaged by Edward Bewley. Here it was intended to establish a farm which would

Some of the surviving buildings at the former Colmanstown model farm, county Galway

act as a model for farms of all sizes, part of it being run as a large farm, part sectioned off as a medium sized farm and part intended to reflect the small farm of ten to fifteen acres or so. Along with the model farm there would be an agricultural school designed to teach the sons of local farmers the skills of agriculture. The preparations for the establishment of the farm included the drainage of some of the land, the diversion of a stream to provide water for a mill and the construction of an extensive range of buildings.

Winding down

As the Colmanstown model farm got under way CRC was winding down its own operations. The great Irish famine was technically over in the autumn of 1849 when the crops survived to feed the people, but in reality it was to be a long time before the country could be said to have returned to normality. The entire economy had been badly affected and the loss of population through death and emigration had been enormous. In May 1849 CRC published an address to the public on behalf of the entire network of Quaker relief workers. This document painted a very bleak picture of the state of Ireland and put forward the proposition that fundamental changes in land law would be the only way of salvaging the country. Even before the publication of the document the first of these changes was under way.

CRC did not cease to exist with the end of the famine. Like the good businessmen that they were, the committee members could not complete their task without a report to its subscribers giving full details as to how the funds were used and giving other pertinent details of the project. The outcome was the 480-page *Transactions of the Central Relief Committee of the Society of Friends during the Famine in Ireland in 1846 and 1847*. The basis for this report was set down by one of the honorary secretaries, Joseph Bewley before his death in September 1851, and shortly afterwards Professor William E. Hearn of Galway College was employed to edit the work. After numerous drafts and consultations the document was published in the autumn of 1852.

During the famine the other honorary secretary, Jonathan Pim, had formed very strong views on the inadequacies of the system of land holding in Ireland and had published a book entitled *Conditions and Prospects of Ireland* (1848) and a pamphlet *Observations on the Evils Resulting to Ireland from the Insecurity of Title and the Existing Laws of Real Property, with Some Suggestions toward a Remedy* (1847). A chapter in *Transactions* also sets down these views, though Jonathan Pim had his doubts as to whether a charitable organisation should be making political comments. This was expressed in the *Transactions*:

> In venturing thus to place before the public our opinions on social and economical questions ... we feel that we are going beyond what some may consider the duty of a committee of a charitable association ... but the circumstances ... have produced in our minds strong convictions of the truth of the principles we advocate, and of their important influence on the future well-being of our country.

The report went on to stress the urgency of the need for change:

> There is no time to lose in effecting these reforms. The present state of the country, while it exhibits some indications of improvement, is such as to cause deep anxiety even to the most hopeful.

The writings and face to face contact with the government throughout the famine had a strong impact on government thinking and led to the passing in 1849 of the first of the new laws to restructure the land system.

Epilogue

The publication of the *Transactions* did not represent the last act of CRC. It ceased to sit as a body, but its work was continued in the model farm at Colmanstown throughout the 1850s. When, in 1862, the state of Ireland was again in turmoil as a result of a bad harvest the surviving members of CRC came together again and co-opted new members to fill the vacancies. In a reflection of the work carried out more than a decade before, they undertook relief measures to reduce the effects of the new famine.

By 1863 this crisis was over and CRC took stock of its future. Apart from some subscription funds remaining in hand, the principal asset was the farm at Colmanstown and it was decided that this venture had outlived its usefulness. The farm was put up for sale and it was decided to donate the proceeds, along with any other funds remaining, to a suitable charity. They selected the Royal Hospital for Incurables, which was non-denominational and was the only institution of its kind in the British Isles. With this final donation, the Central Relief Committee of the Society of Friends laid itself down.

The accounts presented showed that, during their work in the famine, the Dublin and London relief committees had handled just over £200,000 worth of relief, including the costs of transport, but quite apart from clothing. This was not the largest contribution to the Irish famine, the British Relief Association having managed twice as much, and it was just a small part of the total of £1,500,000 donated by private subscribers through various agencies. It also may be compared with some £10 million contributed by the British Exchequer, not including expenditure on arterial drainage and land improvement. The work of Quakers would seem, then, to have been but a minor part of the overall relief operations. The figures are somewhat misleading, however, as they mask the amounts which were recycled by such means as the granting of loans which, when repaid, could be granted again. They also mask the disproportionate effort put in by such a tiny Society (some 3,000 Friends in a population of about 8½ million). On balance, although the sums involved seem small, if translated into today's money they would amount to about £11 million. In addition, the sheer variety of works and the even-handed way in which relief was offered captured the imagination of the people of Ireland who, to this day, have not forgotten that 'the Quakers fed us in the famine'.

The tone of the introduction to the *Transactions* shows that the members of CRC felt that they had not been fully successful in their task. This attitude is understandable in the circumstances as no relief operation could claim to have been a success in the light of such a huge toll of death and emigration. There can be no doubt, however, that many lives were saved and many more were spared from having to emigrate as a direct result of Quaker intervention. This can in no sense be deemed a failure, and if the scale of the task was beyond the reach of such a small group of people, their achievements went far beyond what could have been expected.

Further reading

Robin Goodbody, *A suitable channel: Quaker relief in the Great Famine*, Pale Publishing, 1995.

Helen E. Hatton, *The largest amount of good: Quaker relief in Ireland, 1654-1921*, McGill-Queen's University Press, 1993.

Transactions of the Central Relief Committee of the Society of Friends during the Famine in Ireland in 1846 and 184/, Dublin, 1852.

Society of Friends Relief Papers in the National Archives, Dublin.